Noah Hai

Saturn Re

Methuen Drama

Published by Methuen Drama 2010

1 3 5 7 9 10 8 6 4 2

Methuen Drama
A & C Black Publishers Limited
36 Soho Square
London W1D 3QY
www.methuendrama.com
Copyright © Noah Haidle 2010

Noah Haidle has asserted his rights under the Copyright,
Designs and Patents Act 1988 to be identified as
the author of this work.

ISBN: 978 1 408 14548 7

A CIP catalogue record for this book
is available from the British Library

Typeset by DC Graphic Design Ltd
Printed and bound in Great Britain by
Cox and Whyman Ltd, Reading, Berkshire

Caution

Treasuretrove Productions
in association with Neil McPherson for the Finborough Theatre presents

The European Premiere

Saturn Returns
by Noah Haidle

FINBOROUGH | THEATRE

First Performance at the Finborough Theatre: Tuesday, 2 November 2010
Originally Produced by Lincoln Center Theater, New York City, in 2008

My parents have never been outside of the United States, save for Canada, which doesn't really count since it's across a bridge in Michigan where they live and where I was born and learned why the sky was blue, among other things. My father got his passport just to come to London to see this play. They're quite inconspicuous people, you might be sitting next to them, just listen for the flat a's of the Midwest, especially on words like fire and boat. To get here from Grand Rapids they have to leave their dog Maggie with Trudy, change planes in Chicago and take a ten hour flight, rent a hotel that's not so bad with the pound to dollar ratio, endure the sleepy afternoon of jet-lag, wait quietly for evening among the woo ha of British ambulances, and amble through the often rain upstairs to this theatre.

Most likely your dog is not named Maggie, most likely you did not fly from Grand Rapids, most likely you do not know Trudy who slipped me lollipops when no one was looking. But. Whatever quality of night you have come out of, whatever you call your dog, whatever rhythm your pulse beats, it is my distinct honor that you have done so. Among the sacred things left in the world is the ritual of people joining together to witness a spectacle. And while you most likely have not traveled as far as my parents, you did leave your home, your children, your dog, your bed, your doorframes, your windows, your view.

Home is of course where everyone starts from. And tonight you will most likely return to the softness of familiar pillows. But in between the key closing in the door and the taking off of shoes upon return, for only ninety minutes, your view will be my fever dream, this play you are waiting to see called *Saturn Returns*.

Kurt Vonnegut said you know you are an author when you have an audience of one. And while only one of you is my father, I hope beyond the word that before sleep you are happy you left home for a little bit of time spent together.

Noah Haidle

Saturn Returns

by Noah Haidle

Cast in alphabetical order

Suzanne/Zephyr/Loretta	**Lisa Caruccio Came**
Gustin Novak at 88	**Richard Evans**
Gustin Novak at 58	**Nicholas Gecks**
Gustin Novak at 28	**Christopher Harper**

Director	**Adam Lenson**
Set and Costume Designer	**Bec Chippendale**
Lighting Designer	**James Smith**
Sound Designer	**Sean Ephgrave**
Composer	**Richard Bates**

The performance lasts approximately 80 minutes.

There will be no interval.

Our patrons are respectfully reminded that, in this intimate theatre, any noise
such as rustling programmes, talking or the ringing of mobile phones may
distract the actors and your fellow audience members.

Lisa Caruccio Came
Suzanne/Zephyr/
Loretta

Trained at Tisch
School of The Arts,
New York.

Theatre includes *The Fever Chart* (York Theatre Royal and Trafalgar Studios), *The Woodsman* (Old Red Lion Theatre), *Dark Tales* (Bridewell Theatre and on tour), *Seven Jewish Children* (Hackney Empire), *The Six Wives of Timothy Leary* (Riverside Studios and Pleasance Dome, Edinburgh), *The Dybbuk* (King's Head Theatre), the world premiere of Trevor Griffiths' *Camel Station* (Theatre Museum and Midland Actors Theatre Tour), *The Mothers* (Midland Actors Theatre Tour), *The Time of the Tortoise* (Theatre503), *The Tempest* (The Looking Glass Theater, New York), *A Midsummer Night's Dream* (Lion Theatre, Theater Row, New York), *The Winter's Tale* (Lion Theatre, Theater Row, New York). Film includes *Sprawlers* and *That Samba Thing*.
Radio includes *The Hamam Bride* and *Seeing in the Dark*.

Beowulf (English Shakespeare Company), *As You Like It* (Greenwich Playhouse), *Rosencrantz and Guildenstern Are Dead* (Theatre Royal Bury St Edmunds), two seasons at the Chichester Festival Theatre, *Romeo and Juliet* (London Bubble) *Pickwick Papers Unlawful Killing* (Wolsey Theatre, Ipswich), *Much Ado About Nothing* (Oxford Stage Company), *Julius Caesar* (Royal Exchange Theatre, Manchester), *The Secret Garden* (Library Theatre, Manchester, and National Tour), *Moll Flanders* (Bristol Old Vic), Dominic Cooke's *The Weavers* (Gate Theatre), *Bedroom Farce, Richard IV* (Northcott Theatre, Exeter), *Blavatsky's Tower* (The Flying Machine) and *Under the Greenwood Tree* (Vaudeville Theatre).
Television and Film includes *The Trip, The Conspiracy Theories, The Pinocchio Effect, The Brief, North and South, Fight To The Death, The Gathering, The Inspector Linley Mysteries, One Foot In The Grave, Peak Practice, Between the Lines, Mitch, Rumpole of the Bailey, Dempsey and Makepeace, Auf Wiedersehn Pet* and *Blat*.

Richard Evans Gustin Novak at 88

Recent theatre includes *BookLovers* (King's Head Theatre), *The Crucible* (Bolton Octagon), *Burial At Thebes* (Nottingham Theatre and US Tour), *As You Like It* (Derby Playhouse), *No Shame No Fear* (Jermyn Street Theatre), *Macbeth, Robin Hood* (Creation Theatre), *Open House,* (Riverside Studios), *As You Like It, Antony and Cleopatra* (English Shakespeare Company – National Tour and Perth Festival, Australia),

Nicholas Gecks
Gustin Novak at 58

Theatre includes *The Deep Blue Sea* (Northcott Theatre, Exeter), *The Memory of Water* (National Tour), *Anna Karenina* (Theatre Royal Plymouth), *Night Must Fall* (Theatre Royal Windsor), *Richard II* (National Theatre), *Under the Stars* (Greenwich Theatre), *The Prisoner of Zenda* (Greenwich Theatre), *The Winter's Tale* (Royal Exchange Theatre, Manchester), *Lady Windermere's Fan* (Watford Palace Theatre), *A Patriot for Me* (Chichester Festival Theatre,

West End and Los Angeles), *The Beaux Stratagem, A Midsummer Night's Dream, The Accrington Pals, Suicide, Nicholas Nickleby, The Merry Wives of Windsor, Cymbeline, Julius Caesar, Baal* (all Royal Shakespeare Company).

Television includes *Doctors, Collision, Doctor Who, Inspector Lynley, Sea of Souls, Lazarus Child, Red Cap, Scarlet Pimpernel, The Dark Room, Between the Lines, Secret Agent, Not A Penny More Not A Penny Less, Pirates, The Marlowe Inquest, Mrs Capper's Birthday, A Still Small Shout, Titus Andronicus, Prisoner of Zenda, The Falklands Factor, Crack in the Ice, East Lynne, Julius Caesar, A Face at the Window, Children of the North, Sherlock, The Forsyte Saga, The Return of Sherlock Holmes, Othello, Coronation Street, Seeing Red, Brookside, The Mill on the Floss, Richard II, The Chief, Wycliffe, Berlin Break, Sherlock Holmes and the Leading Lady, The Bill, Making News, Hunted Down, Chekov in Yalta, Rumpole of the Bailey, The Grand Tour, Six Centuries of Verse, Wolf to the Slaughter, Two Per Cent, Nicholas Nickleby* and *Reilly Ace of Spies*.

Film includes *Mutant Chronicles, Parting Shots, Richard II, Tai Pan, Forever Young, To the Lighthouse* and *The Wicked Lady*.

Christopher Harper
Gustin Novak at 28

Theatre includes *Light Shining in Buckinghamshire* (Arcola Theatre), *Journey's End* (National Tour), *After Miss Julie, People at Sea* (Salisbury Playhouse), *Man of the Moment, Private Fears in Public Places* (Northampton Royal Theatre), *Twelfth Night* (Thelma Holt Productions), *Much Ado About Nothing* (Sprite Productions), *Lie of the Land* (Arcola Theatre), *See How They Run, Separate Tables, Volpone* (Royal Exchange Theatre, Manchester), *Strange Orchestra, Adam Bede* (Orange Tree Theatre, Richmond), *You Were After Poetry, Assembly* (HighTide) and *Tabloid Caligula* (Arcola Theatre and New York).

TV includes *Upstairs Downstairs, Doctors, The Bill, Heartbeat,* Cliff Last in Victoria Wood's *Housewife 49, Rosemary and Thyme, The Roman Mysteries* and *Life on Mars*.

Film includes Bollywood film *Patiala House* and *Rules of the Game* which was nominated for awards at Cannes and Raindance in 2009.

Noah Haidle Playwright
Playwright Noah Haidle is one of America's most exciting young writers and "a name to watch" (*LA Times*). *Saturn Returns* marks his UK debut, and he is working directly with the director to develop and expand the piece for this London staging. *Saturn Returns* was first produced in 2008 at Lincoln Center Theater, New York City. His other work includes *Persephone* (Huntington Theater Company, University of Boston), *Vigils* (Goodman Theatre, Chicago, and Woolly Mammoth Theatre Company, Washington DC), *Mr. Marmalade* (Roundabout Theatre, New York, and South Coast Repertory, California), *Princess Marjorie* (South Coast Repertory, California) and *Rag and Bone* (Long Wharf Theatre, Connecticut). He has taught playwriting at Princeton University, the Kennedy Center and in Kenya and Uganda as part of The Sundance Theatre Institute. He is a graduate of Princeton University and The Juilliard School, where he was a Lila Acheson Wallace Playwright-in-Residence.

He is the recipient of three Lincoln Center Le Compte Du Nouy Awards, the 2005 Helen Merrill Award for emerging playwrights, the 2007 Claire Tow Award, and an NEA/TCG theatre residency grant. He lives in Brooklyn, New York City.

Adam Lenson Director
Theatre at the Finborough Theatre includes the UK premieres of *Ordinary Days* (2008), *Little Fish* (2009) and Nick Payne's *Adam Lives in Theory* as part of *Vibrant – An Anniversary Festival of Finborough Playwrights* (2010).
Trained at Cambridge University and on the National Theatre Studio Directors' Course.
Directing includes *The Family* (Public Theater, New York), *Immaculate* (Etcetera Theatre), *The Rain King* (Start Night at Hampstead Theatre), *Hades* (The Company Project at Theatre503), *Bifurcated* (Nabakov Present Tense at Southwark Playhouse), *Cell Begat Cell* (Symposium at The Old Vic) and *These Memories Must Go* (24 Hour Plays at The Old Vic).
Assistant and Resident Directing includes *The Prisoner of Second Avenue* (Vaudeville Theatre), *Six Degrees of Separation* (The Old Vic), *An Inspector Calls* (West End and National Tour), *La Cage aux Folles* (Menier Chocolate Factory and West End), *Talent* (Menier Chocolate Factory) and *The Music Man* (Chichester Festival Theatre).

Bec Chippendale Set and Costume Design
At the Finborough Theatre, Bec designed *Ordinary Days* (2008) and *Little Fish* (2009).
Trained in Theatre Design at Wimbledon School of Art
Theatre includes *The House on the Backwater* (Hen and Chickens Theatre), *Hitting Town* (Canterbury), *The Rimers of Eldritch* (Edinburgh Festival) and *Little Shop of Horrors* (Dorset).
As an Assistant Designer, she has worked on *The Wizard of Oz* (London Palladium), *The King and I* (Royal Albert Hall), *Cyrano de Bergerac* (Chichester Festival Theatre), *Calendar Girls* (Chichester Festival Theatre and National Tour), *The Sound of Music* (London Palladium and Toronto), *A Voyage Round My Father* (Donmar Warehouse and Wyndham's Theatre), *Rock 'n' Roll* (Royal Court and Duke of York's Theatre), *On the Town* (London Coliseum), *Guillo Cesare* (Glyndebourne), *Cloaca* (Old Vic), *L'Incoronazione di Popea* (Champs-Elysees Opera), *Marty* (Boston), *The Dance of Death* (Lyric Theatre), *Miserly Knight and Gianni Schicchi* (Glyndebourne), *Three Sisters* and *Jumpers* (National Theatre).
Television and Film work includes Art Director on *Hamlet* (Royal Shakespeare Company, Illuminations and BBC), Production Designer on *About Turn*, Art Director on *Can't Buy Me Love*, Art Department on *The Last Chancers* and as a Model Maker for *Die Another Day*.

James Smith Lighting Designer
At the Finborough Theatre, James was Lighting Designer for *Ordinary Days* (2008), *Untitled* (2009), *Painting a Wall* (2009), *Death of Long Pig* (2009), *Little Fish* (2009) and Lingua Franca (and its subsequent transfer to 59E59 Theaters, Off-Broadway)
Theatre includes *Fame the Musical* (National Tour), *Keeping Up Appearances* (National Tour), *Alf Ramsey Knew My Grandfather* (Theatre Royal, Newcastle), *Cinderella* (Derby Assembly Rooms), *Artist Descending a Staircase* (Old Red

Lion Theatre), *Till I Die* and *Bed Time Solos* (Old Red Lion Theatre and Octagon Theatre, Bolton), *The Heat is On!* (Bournemouth Pier Theatre and National Tour), *The Extra Factor* (National Tour), *Cinderella* (Hackney Empire), *Sweet Charity* (Stratford, London), *One Flew Over The Cuckoo's Nest* (BAC), *Picture Perfect* (National Tour) and various productions for Haringey Shed Theatre Company, Stage Coach, Stageworks Theatre School and Hackney Empire. Future Lighting Designs for 2010 include lighting aboard Cunard's newest ocean liner, *The Queen Elizabeth*, the Off Broadway transfer of *Snow White* (Shaw Theatre) and *Motherhood The Musical* (King's Theatre Glasgow) *Aladdin* (Derby Assembly Rooms).

James has designed for corporate clients internationally including the Volkswagen Group, GlaxoSmithKline and Sony, and most recently Liverpool Victoria and the BBC.

James works as an Associate Lighting Designer to both Mark Jonathan and Howard Harrison. Recent projects include *Flashdance* (Shaftesbury Theatre), *Curtains* (Guildhall School of Music and Drama), *Inherit The Wind* (The Old Vic), *The Music Man* (Chichester Festival Theatre), *Jane Eyre* (London Children's Ballet), *The Circle* (Chichester Festival Theatre and National Tour) and *Nicholas Nickleby* (Chichester Festival Theatre, London and National Tour). Other projects as Assistant Lighting Designer include *Babes in Arms* (Chichester Festival Theatre), *Macbeth* (Chichester Festival Theatre and Gielgud Theatre), *The Wizard of Oz* (Birmingham Rep), *Skellig* (Young Vic) and *Suddenly Last Summer* (Crucible Theatre, Sheffield, and National

Tour). His latest relights are for *Tracy Beaker Gets Real* (Nottingham Playhouse and National Tour), *London Assurance* (Watermill Theatre, Newbury, and National Tour*), She Stoops to Conquer, Dangerous Liaisons* (Mappa Mundi Theatre Company).

James also works as a freelance lecturer in Lighting Design and Lighting Management at Rose Bruford College.

Sean Ephgrave Sound Designer
At the Finborough Theatre, Sean was Sound Designer on *Little Fish* (2009). Trained at the Central School of Speech and Drama.

Sound Designs include *The Local Stigmatic* (Barons Court Theatre), *Music Lessons* and *Twelfth Night* (Embassy Theatre), *The Speculator* (Embassy Studio) and *Fundamental* (Arts Depot).

Associate Sound Designs include *All About My Mother, Branded* (The Old Vic), *The Lover and The Collection* (Comedy Theatre), *The City* (Royal Court Theatre), *Testing The Echo* and *Anderson's English* (Out of Joint), *The Country Wife* (Theatre Royal Haymarket), and *The Little Dog Laughed* (Garrick Theatre).

Sean also works extensively at the National Theatre and has worked as opening sound operator on *The Revenger's Tragedy, Her Naked Skin, Oedipus* (all at the Olivier Theatre) and *Women of Troy* (Lyttleton Theatre).

Richard Bates Composer
Studied composition with Michael Finissy and Giles Swayne, and has participated in seminars led by John Rutter, Howard Skempton and John Woolrich.

He regularly composes choral music for The Platinum Consort, who most recently premiered his *Tenebrae*

Responsories in a London music festival in June. In addition to his work on *Saturn Returns,* Richard is also in the final stages of preparing his musical *Animate* for a West End reading at the end of November. Richard also regularly works as Music Director on numerous London productions, including, most recently, the world premiere of the musical of *Remains Of The Day,* based on the novel by Kazuo Ishiguro (Union Theatre). Future productions include *1888: A London Mystery.*
Richard also works as a Musical Director with numerous credits including the world premiere of a musical version of Remains of the Day, based on the novel by Kazuo Ishiguro (Union Theatre). Future productions include *1888: A London Mystery.*

Bethan Dear Assistant Director
At the Finborough Theatre, Bethan is a Resident Assistant Director and has assisted on *Love on the Dole, His Greatness* and, as part of *Vibrant – An Anniversary Festival of Finborough Playwrights; Beating Heart Cadaver, Lights in the Sky, Rock, Paper, Scissors* and *The Voice of Scotland* (2010). Trained at Middlesex University. Previous productions include *Mad Forest, The Raft of the Medusa* and *The Insect Play* (Middlesex University).

Joshua Black Producer
Studied at the University of Cambridge. Producing includes *Diary of a Lost Boy* (White Bear Theatre), *Prophesy* (Public Theater, New York), *Scapegoats* (Tik sho-ret Theatre Company), *Symposium* (The Old Vic), *Assassins* (Landor Theatre), *Sweeney Todd: The Demon Barber of Fleet Street* (C too Edinburgh), *Waiting for Godot* and *Folk* (Horseshoe Theatre Company, Cambridge).

Assisting credits include *A Man of No Importance* (Union Theatre and the Arts Theatre) and *Out of the Piano* (Cochrane Theatre) *Oklahoma!* (Cambridge Arts Theatre).
Joshua was one of the producers on the Old Vic New Voices T.S. Eliot US/UK Exchange 2010.

Hanna Osmolska Producer
Producing and General Management includes the world premiere of the 'lost' John Osborne play, *Personal Enemy* (London and Brits Off Broadway, New York), the West End transfer of *Madness in Valencia* (Trafalgar Studios 2), *Mummies and Daddies* (White Bear Theatre), *Pause to Wonder* (ADC Theatre and Hen and Chickens, London) Black and White Rainbow's *InSite* (site specific), *Oklahoma!* (Cambridge Arts Theatre), *Twelfth Night* (US Tour), and *under the blue, blue moon* (Edinburgh Festival and National Tour).
Hanna was one of the producers on the Old Vic New Voices T.S. Eliot US/UK Exchange 2010, and is currently undertaking the Stage One Apprenticeship.

Production Acknowledgements
Production Manager | **David Neill**
Stage Manager | **Chiara Canal**
Assistant Director | **Bethan Dear**
Press Representative | **Finborough Theatre 07977 173135**
Producers | **Joshua Black and Hanna Osmolska**

With thanks to
Charlotte Bevan, Michael Callahan at Josef Weinberger, Thea Foster, Corinne Hayoun and Jeff Augustin at Creative Artists Agency (CAA), Terry Johnson, Ava Morgan, The Old Vic, Damian Robertson, Himesh Sheth. Rehearsal space provided by the National Youth Theatre.

FINBOROUGH | THEATRE

Theatre presents plays and music theatre, concentrating exclusively on new writing and rediscoveries from the 19th and 20th centuries. Behind the scenes, we continue to discover and develop a new generation of theatre makers – through our vibrant Literary Department, our hugely successful internship programme, our Resident Assistant Director Programme, and our partnership with the National Theatre Studio – the Leverhulme Bursary for Emerging Directors.

Despite remaining completely unfunded, the Finborough Theatre has an unparalleled track record of discovering new playwrights who go on to become leading voices in British theatre. Under Artistic Director Neil McPherson, it has discovered some of the UK's most exciting new playwrights including Laura Wade, James Graham, Mike Bartlett, Sarah Grochala, Jack Thorne, Joy Wilkinson, Simon Vinnicombe, Alexandra Wood, Al Smith, Nicholas de Jongh and Anders Lustgarten.

"One of the most stimulating venues in London, fielding a programme that is a bold mix of trenchant, politically thought-provoking new drama and shrewdly chosen revivals of neglected works from the past." *The Independent*

"A disproportionately valuable component of the London theatre ecology. Its programme combines new writing and revivals, in selections intelligent and audacious." *Financial Times*

"A blazing beacon of intelligent endeavour, nurturing new writers while finding and reviving neglected curiosities from home and abroad." *The Daily Telegraph*

"The pocket-size Finborough Theatre, under the artistic direction of Neil McPherson, has been earning a place on the must-visit list with its eclectic, smartly curated slate of new works and neglected masterpieces" *Vogue*

Celebrating its 30th anniversary in 2010, the multi-award-winning Finborough

Founded in 1980, artists working at the theatre in the 1980's included Clive Barker, Rory Bremner, Nica Burns, Kathy Burke, Ken Campbell, Jane Horrocks and Claire Dowie. In the 1990's, the Finborough Theatre became particularly known for new writing including Naomi Wallace's first play *The War Boys*; Rachel Weisz in David Farr's *Neville Southall's Washbag*; four plays by Anthony Neilson including *Penetrator* and *The Censor*, both of which transferred to the Royal Court Theatre; and new plays by Tony Marchant, David Eldridge, Mark Ravenhill and Phil Willmott. New writing development included a number of works that went to become modern classics including Mark Ravenhill's *Shopping and F***king*, Conor McPherson's *This Lime Tree Bower*, Naomi Wallace's *Slaughter City* and Martin McDonagh's *The Pillowman*.

Since 2000, new British plays have included Laura Wade's London debut with her adaptation of W.H. Davies' *Young Emma*, commissioned for the Finborough Theatre; Simon Vinnicombe's *Year 10* which went on to play at BAC's *Time Out* Critics' Choice Season; James Graham's

Albert's Boy with Victor Spinetti; Sarah Grochala's *S27*; Nigel Planer's *Death of Long Pig*; Peter Nichols' *Lingua Franca*; Joy Wilkinson's *Fair*, Nicholas de Jongh's *Plague Over England* and Jack Thorne's *Fanny and Faggot,* all of which transferred to the West End. Many of the Finborough Theatre's new plays have been published and are on sale from our website.

UK premieres of foreign plays have included Brad Fraser's *Wolfboy*; Lanford Wilson's *Sympathetic Magic*; Larry Kramer's *The Destiny of Me*; Tennessee Williams' *Something Cloudy, Something Clear*; the English premiere of Robert McLellan's Scots language classic, *Jamie the Saxt*; and three West transfers – Frank McGuinness' *Gates of Gold* with William Gaunt and John Bennett, Joe DiPietro's *F***ing Men* and Craig Higginson's *Dream of the Dog* with Janet Suzman.

Rediscoveries of neglected work have included the first London revivals of Rolf Hochhuth's *Soldiers* and *The Representative*; both parts of Keith Dewhurst's *Lark Rise to Candleford*; *The Women's War*, an evening of original suffragette plays; *Etta Jenks* with Clarke Peters and Daniela Nardini; Noël Coward's first play, *The Rat Trap*; Charles Wood's *Jingo* with Susannah Harker; the sell-out production of Patrick Hamilton's *Hangover Square*; and the *Time Out* Critics' Choice revival of J.M. Barrie's *What Every Woman Knows*.

Music Theatre has included the new (premieres from Grant Olding, Charles Miller, Michael John LaChuisa, Adam Guettel, Andrew Lippa and Adam Gwon) and the old (the UK premiere of Rodgers and Hammerstein's *State Fair* which transferred to the West End, and the acclaimed *Celebrating British Music Theatre* series, reviving forgotten British musicals).

The Finborough Theatre won the Empty Space Peter Brook Mark Marvin Award in 2004; and won the inaugural Empty Space Peter Brook Award's prestigious Dan Crawford Pub Theatre Award in 2005 and again in 2008. It is the only theatre without public funding to be awarded the prestigious Pearson Playwriting Award bursary for writers Chris Lee in 2000, Laura Wade (also for Pearson Award Best Play) in 2005 (who also went on to win the Critics' Circle Theatre Award for Most Promising Playwright, the George Devine Award and an Olivier Award nomination), for James Graham (also for Pearson Award Best Play) in 2006, for Al Smith in 2007, for Anders Lustgarten in 2009 and Simon Vinnicombe in 2010. Former Literary Manager Alexandra Wood also won the George Devine Award in 2007. Neil McPherson won the Best Artistic Director award at the 2009 Fringe Report Awards.

www.finboroughtheatre.co.uk

FINBOROUGH | THEATRE

118 Finborough Road, London
SW10 9ED
admin@finboroughtheatre.co.uk
www.finboroughtheatre.co.uk

Artistic Director | **Neil McPherson**
Resident Designer | **Alex Marker**
General Manager | **Sanne Berntsen,
Holly Chivers**
Pearson Playwright-in-Residence | **Simon
Vinnicombe**
Playwrights-in-Residence | **Bekah
Brunstetter, James Graham, Anders
Lustgarten**
Literary Manager | **Van Badham**
Literary Assistant | **Daniel Burgess**
Leverhulme Director in Residence in
association with the National Theatre Studio
| **Ria Parry**
Associate Artist | **Eleanor Rhode**
Associate Producer | **Benn Cody**
Marketing | **Gemma Bealing**
Casting Associate | **Rachel Payant**
Casting Assistant | **Hayley Kaimakliotis**
Resident Assistant Director | **Bethan Dear**

The Finborough Theatre has the support
of the Pearson Playwrights' Scheme.
Sponsored by Pearson PLC.

The Leverhulme Bursary for Emerging
Directors is a partnership between the
National Theatre Studio and the Finborough
Theatre, supported by The Leverhulme
Trust.

The Finborough Theatre is a member of
the Independent Theatre Council, Musical
Theatre Matters UK (MTM:UK) and The
Earl's Court Society www.earlscourtsociety.
org.uk

Ecovenue

Ecovenue is a European Regional
Development Fund backed three year
initiative of The Theatres Trust, aiming to
improve the environmental sustainability
of 48 small to medium sized performing
arts spaces across London. www.ecovenue.
org.uk

Online
Join us at Facebook, Twitter, MySpace and
YouTube.

Mailing
Email admin@finboroughtheatre.co.uk or
give your details to our Box Office staff to
join our free email list. If you would like to
be sent a free season leaflet every three
months, just include your postal address
and postcode.

Feedback
We welcome your comments, complaints
and suggestions. Write to Finborough
Theatre, 118 Finborough Road, London
SW10 9ED or email us at admin@
finboroughtheatre.co.uk

Friends
The Finborough Theatre is a registered
charity. We receive no public funding, and
rely solely on the support of our audiences.
Please do consider supporting us by
becoming a member of our Friends of the
Finborough Theatre scheme. There are
four categories of Friends, each offering a
wide range of benefits.
Richard Tauber Friends – Charles Lascelles.
Lionel Monckton Friends – Anonymous.
Philip and Christine Carne. Stephen Harper.
William Terriss Friends – Tom Erhardt.
Leo and Janet Liebster. Peter Lobl. Bhagat
Sharma.

Smoking is not permitted in the auditorium
and the use of cameras and recording
equipment is strictly prohibited.

In accordance with the requirements of the
Royal Borough of Kensington and Chelsea:

1. The public may leave at the end of
   the performance by all doors and such
   doors must at that time be kept open.

2. All gangways, corridors, staircases and external passageways intended for exit shall be left entirely free from obstruction whether permanent or temporary.
3. Persons shall not be permitted to stand or sit in any of the gangways intercepting the seating or to sit in any of the other gangways.

The Finborough Theatre is licensed by the Royal Borough of Kensington and Chelsea to The Steam Industry, a registered charity and a company limited by guarantee. Registered in England no. 3448268. Registered Charity no. 1071304. Registered Office: 118 Finborough Road, London SW10 9ED. The Steam Industry is under the Artistic Direction of Phil Willmott. www. philwillmott.co.uk

Air Conditioning Appeal

We are currently fundraising for air conditioning for the auditorium.
We are a completely unfunded registered charity. We have made many fundraising applications for the £10,000 that we need for a complete air conditioning system, but have been unsuccessful to date.
If you would like to make a donation towards the installation of air conditioning, do please speak to any member of the Box Office Staff.

Saturn Returns

For Jerry, who threw me to the wolves

WHO'S WHO

Gustin, glasses, a moustache, slightly hunched. We see him at ages 28, 58, and 88 and for clarity's sake that's how he'll be noted. The glasses might get thicker, the moustache greyer and the hunch more.

Suzanne, a nurse.

Zephyr, Gustin's daughter.

Loretta, Gustin's wife.

Suzanne, Zephyr, and Loretta are all played by the same actress in her late twenties.

PLACE AND TIME

A living room in Frankfort, Michigan. We see it over the course of sixty years and over that time is has greatly decayed.

The play is performed without an intermission.

Scene One

A living room in Frankfort, Michigan.
Not looking so good. That's an understatement.
Dirty rugs. Some plastic covers on the furniture. Wallpaper falling off.
The only architectural matter to consider is an entrance to the kitchen.
A closet.
A front door.
We're close enough to the water so that we can hear the waves breaking.
And a staircase up to the bedrooms. The staircase is important.
88 *sits cross-legged on the ground.*
The nurse is feeling his heartbeat with a stethoscope.
She is in work clothes. He is in pajamas which don't look so good either.

88 Still beating is it?

Suzanne It is.

88 You look just like my daughter.
That other girl they sent looked like a horse.

Suzanne Cheryl is a friend of mine.

88 Excuse me.
You are friends with a girl with a horse face.

Suzanne I'm not her.

88 No.
You look just like my daughter and my daughter is beautiful.

Suzanne Does she live close?

88 Not anymore.

Suzanne Or else she could take care of you.

88 Or else she could.

Suzanne Your blood pressure is fine.
Your eyes are good.
Your hearing is perfect.

88 What?

Suzanne   Your hearing.
That was a joke.

88   I still got it.

Suzanne   You don't have a problem with your bowel
movements.

88   Or taking a piss.

Suzanne   Or urination.

88   I'm eighty-eight years old and I still piss standing up.

Suzanne   You're perfectly healthy.

88   You said it.

Suzanne   I don't know why you need an assisted living
professional.

88   I don't.

Suzanne   Why did you call me?

88   Because Cheryl had the face of a horse.

Suzanne   Sir?

88   It's a remarkable resemblance.
If we were to walk down the street, on our way to the post
office to mail a letter, people would do double takes and say to
themselves that is his daughter.

Suzanne   You didn't answer my question.

88   Can you make scrambled eggs?
Of course you can.
Everybody can.

Suzanne   Dr. (*Checks sheet.*) Novak.

88   I am quite famished.

Suzanne   Sir.

88   A bit of grapefruit juice would help my throat.

Suzanne   Sir, I'm going to call my service and say I am not needed here.

She packs up her bag.

88   You are.

Suzanne   Excuse me.

88   You are.
Needed.
Here.

Suzanne   But you're fine.

88   She's dead.

Suzanne   Who is dead?

88   My daughter.
She used to make me scrambled eggs and grapefruit juice.
Could you do that?
And then you can go.
Will you make me breakfast?

Suzanne   Okay. I'll make you breakfast.

88   There's nobody you can call.
I looked in the phone book.
I called the plumber, Larry, but my toilet was fine so I plugged it up with a tennis ball.
And he got it out and said how did a tennis ball get in your toilet and I couldn't think of a lie so I told him, Larry, I put it there myself.
And he said why did you put a tennis ball in your toilet and I said have you ever been lonely?
And he said no and he left.
I didn't believe him.
About the lonely part.
I've called other people.
There are lots of numbers in the phone book.
I called an au pair but my daughter is grown up and dead anyway.

I called the suicide hotline but I'm not suicidal.
I called an escort, Cinnamon, but I haven't had an erection in years.
I called Cheryl but she looked like a horse.
And then I called you.
Please don't go.
I don't have anybody else to call.

Suzanne   I'll stay.

88   I just want somebody to talk to.

Suzanne   What do you want to say?

88   It wasn't a particular conversation I had in mind.
I have little talent for small talk.
Maybe you could tell me about yourself.
Let's start with your name.

Suzanne   My name is Suzanne.

88   I had a cousin named Suzanne.
Never a more foul-smelling cross-eyed bitch did I ever meet.
But the name suits you fine.

Suzanne   I grew up here in Frankfort.

88   I grew old here.

Suzanne   I went to Frankfort High.

88   So did I.
But we probably didn't go at the same time.

Suzanne   Probably not.

88   I was on the baseball team.

Suzanne   I wasn't.

88   No, I wouldn't think so.
They say I could have gone professional.

Suzanne   Why didn't you?

88   They were wrong.
Where did you live?

Suzanne   Our house was on Sherman Street.

88   Not on Sherman.

Suzanne   Across from the hospital.

88   I worked at the hospital.

Suzanne   What did you do?

88   I was a radiologist.

Suzanne   I broke my arm once.
Ned Hefron pushed me from the swings because I wouldn't
tongue kiss him.

88   It could have been me who read your x-ray.

Suzanne   It could have been.

88   Have you broken any other bones?

Suzanne   No.

88   Too bad.

Suzanne   Just the arm.

88   Because it would have given us a higher probability of
having met.
But maybe I saw you out my window.
Playing in the front yard.
Or learning to ride a bicycle on the street.
I might have seen you every day out my window.
Maybe I was a witness to your life.

Suzanne   How did your daughter die?

88   Does it matter?

Suzanne   I would like to know.

88   I'm a bit hungry. My throat. Quite parched.

Suzanne   Please.

88   I don't exactly talk about her.

Suzanne   What about your wife?
Where is she?

88   What?
Are you talking?

Suzanne   What was her name at least?

88   I hear a voice.
It's so far away.

Suzanne   Your daughter.
What was your daughter's name?

88   Zephyr.

Suzanne   Like the west wind.

88   Like the west wind.
It was her mother's idea to name her that but I don't speak of
her so my daughter was named Zephyr.
And she was about your age and one day she wasn't alive
anymore.
Can I have some eggs please?

Suzanne   That's not the whole story.

88   No shit.
The whole story is too long to tell.
It's raising a girl yourself and living and loving her and then
her dying in the ocean near Mexico and getting a coffin
through customs is no joke but it's not her body it's a one-eyed
Mexican named Manuel and then losing your daughter's body
and finding her in East Africa and they didn't refrigerate her so
by the time she gets to you she smells like four-day-old farts or
worse and the airline giving you free tickets for life so you can
fly anywhere for free but the problem is you have nowhere to
go and worse no one to go with no it's not the whole story it's
not even close.

Suzanne   Is that a true story?

88   You think I could make that up?

Suzanne   If you wanted.

88   Even the part about Manuel, the one-eyed Mexican?

Suzanne   If you want, you can make anything up.

88   If I made anything up I'd make up a story where Zephyr
didn't go to Mexico.
That I didn't let her go.
That I didn't have to bury her next to her mother who I do
not talk about and how I wouldn't find out that no matter how
much you cry there is no end to tears.
You'd think after awhile it would dry up.
But there is no end to them.
I've waited for the end.
But it won't come.
Not yet.
I've waited.
I'm still waiting.
I can't help but wait.

Suzanne   Maybe I'll make your breakfast now.

88   I am quite famished.

Suzanne   Scrambled eggs.

88   But not too runny.

Suzanne   Not too runny.

88   But not too firm.

Suzanne   Right in the middle.

88   Right in the middle.

Suzanne   And some grapefruit juice.

88   My throat is quite parched.

Suzanne   I'll get it for you.

88   Thank you.
What's your name again?

Suzanne   Suzanne.

88   That's right.
Thank you, Suzanne.
I've waited so long for somebody to make me breakfast.

Suzanne   You don't have to wait anymore.
I'll be back in no time.

88   I'll be waiting right here.

She goes into the kitchen.

88   I'll be waiting.

He puts his head into his hands and cries.
Lights fade.

Scene Two

The same living room.
Thirty years earlier. The plastic is off the furniture and the wallpaper is not peeling but there is a worn feeling to the place.
It is morning.
58 *sits cross-legged on the ground.*
Zephyr *calls from where the nurse exited. It's the same actress so this gives her a little time to change.*

Zephyr (*offstage*)   Dad?
Are you awake?

58   Is there a difference anymore?

Zephyr (*offstage*)   There is every bit of difference.

58   So you say.
I remain unconvinced.

Zephyr *enters.*
She's got heavy eye makeup and her hair is different. She's eclectically unkempt.
They kiss.

58   You look just like your mother except for the hair.

Zephyr   Are we talking about Mom today?

58   Did I say we were?
We're talking about that haircut.

Zephyr   What?
It's new.

58   I like the old one.

Zephyr   It's very fashionable.

58   You look like you work in a carnival.

Zephyr   Are you the world's expert on what carnival workers' hair looks like?

58   I am near the top of the field, yes.

They smile.

Zephyr   We need to get ready for the Bonnie situation.

58   Is that her name this time?

Zephyr   It is her name.

58   I'm hungry.

Zephyr   You don't get breakfast until we talk about Bonnie.

58   I have to go to work.

Zephyr   You're fine for time.

58   People have broken bones.

Zephyr   They'll still be broken when you get there.

She takes out a sheet with a picture.

Zephyr   Now.
Bonnie is a piano teacher.

58   I hate the piano.

Zephyr   Since when.

58   Since it doesn't matter I hate it.

Zephyr   So she won't play the piano.
It's not like you have to take lessons.

58   But she'll talk about the piano.
About giving lessons to pimply twelve-year-olds and about
Chopin and about Debussy and don't you think Mozart is a
little overrated?

Zephyr   So change the subject.

58   To what?

Zephyr   It doesn't matter.
This is a first date.

58   They're all first dates.

Zephyr   And the point of a first date is to get to a second
date.
And the point of a second date is to get to a third date and
then to you know what and then to be happy.

58   You're talking to me about being happy.

Zephyr   I am.

58   She's talking to me about being happy.

Zephyr   Now about Bonnie.

58   "Do you like Chopin's preludes?"
"They're so evocative."
She'll use words like that.
If she says evocative I'm leaving.

Zephyr   You can't leave.

58   I can and I will.

Zephyr   That hurt Meredith's feelings.

58   Oh, I'm sorry.

Zephyr   You said you were going to the bathroom and you didn't come back.

58   And.

Zephyr   And that's very rude.
She called me crying.

58   She wouldn't stop talking about birds migrating.
What do I care about birds migrating?

Zephyr   Because it's important to her.

58   Birds leave.
They come back.
Hooray!

Zephyr   What about Toni?

58   Her name sounds like somebody who hangs drywall.

Zephyr   Virginia?

58   I had a bad experience in Roanoke. And she smelled like roast beef.

Zephyr   You had a bad experience in Roanoke and her name was Virginia so you didn't ask her out again. And nobody smells like roast beef.

58   I swear. Four-day-old roast beef, like roast beef you left in a hot closet.

Zephyr   What was the nature of this bad experience in Roanoke?

58   Let's just say it involved Jose Cuervo Gold a mechanical bull and a spastic colon.

Zephyr   You make up these stories just to spite me.

58   No, I make them up to amuse myself.
There's no one else to do it.
So I do it myself.

Zephyr   You've never been to Roanoke, have you?

58   Not to my knowledge.

Zephyr   So Virginia.

58   She wasn't your mother.

Zephyr   Nobody is!

58   Which is exactly my point.
Find a way to resurrect her and we'll talk.

Zephyr   Back to Bonnie.

58   Is that her name this time?

Zephyr   It is her name.
And she's the last one.

58   Good.

Zephyr   That's not good.
There isn't anybody else to call.

58   I've run through the lot of them.

Zephyr   I've asked everybody I know.
You need to take this one seriously.

58   No problem.
Bonnie.
Bonnie.
Sounds like a great big fat person.

Zephyr   You're not taking this seriously.

58   This is me being serious.

Zephyr   So what if she is on the plus side?

58   What do you know?

Zephyr   Her cousin gave me a picture.

58   Is she a great big fat person?

Zephyr   She's not small.

He takes the picture.

58   Not small?
She's a heifer not small.

Zephyr   That's an old picture.
She may have lost some weight.

58   Or gained more.
Jesus.
She probably has her own zip code.

Zephyr   Dad.
Stop.

58   Okay.
I stopped.

Zephyr   Bonnie sounds like a very nice person.

58   Fantastic. And isn't that exactly what they always say about fat people? I stopped.

Zephyr   Let's practice your small talk.
So.
I hear it's going to snow.

58   Are you a private investigator, Bonnie?
How did you possibly deduce this information?
Was it the world growing colder again?
Reminding me of the absence of my light?

Zephyr   Okay.
No weather.

58   No weather whatsoever.

Zephyr   Have you heard any good jokes lately?

58   And what are jokes to you, Bonnie?
A little ha ha in a night?
Here's a joke for you.
Did you ever hear the one about the man who thought he
could hold onto his happiness?

Zephyr   This isn't small talk at all!

58   Did you ever feel it belonged to you?
Huh?
Do you have an opinion on that subject, Bonnie?
DO YOU THINK YOU CAN OWN YOUR HAPPINESS??

Zephyr   You're totally going to freak her out.

58   So be it.

Zephyr   I don't know why I bother.

58   Neither do I.

Zephyr   I spend time on this.

58   I never asked you to.

Zephyr   No, you never asked.
But I want you to get out.

58   What's out there?

Zephyr   Other people.

58   What do I need other people for?

Zephyr   You're still young.

58   Not that young anymore.
I'm 58.

Zephyr   I just want you to have somebody.

58   I have you.

Zephyr   But I won't be around forever.

58   Where are you going?

Zephyr   You can't expect me to play wet nurse forever.

58   Nothing lasts forever.

Zephyr   Oh good, nothing lasts forever.
Can we put that on a t-shirt and sell it at a rock concert?

58   It's true.

Zephyr   True or not, what are we doing?
Selling Hallmark cards.
Nothing lasts forever.
And every day, every minute you think of her.
And no, I never met her.
But.
If you treated her like you treat me she would have left, too.

He slaps her.

58   I'm sorry.

Zephyr   No, it's okay.

58   I didn't mean to touch you.

Zephyr   You better get to work.

58   Will you accept my apology?

Zephyr   Sure.

58   Fully accepted?

Zephyr   Fully.

58   Listen, I'll take this Bonnie situation seriously.
Okay?
I'll ask her her favorite song and I'll sing it.
And I'll say how her dress is so wonderfully slimming.
Okay?
Is that what you want?

Zephyr   I just want you to be happy.

58   Too late for that.

Zephyr   It's not too late for that!!

58   You can't replace your mother.

Zephyr   I'm not trying to replace her.

58   Because you can't.

Zephyr   I just can't take care of you anymore.

58   Okay.
I can clean up.

He cleans.

58   I can cook for myself.
From now on I'm the one who makes you breakfast.
How about that?
No one can poach an egg like me.
Hash browns. Famous.
A banana?
What do you want?
A little breakfast to begin the day!

He begins to go.

Zephyr   No.
Dad.

58   A waffle?
Legendary.
A waffle with sausage links.
A real lumberjack breakfast!

Zephyr   Stop.

58   Where is Bonnie that hefty bitch?

Zephyr   Stop it, Dad.

58   I stopped.
Okay?
I stopped.
Take a trip.

Somewhere warm.
Take a break from me and then you'll come home.
It will be beautiful.
There's nothing more beautiful than a homecoming.

Zephyr   You're going to be late for work.

58   Maybe later.
Maybe later today we can talk about your mother.

Zephyr   I'll make you breakfast.

58   You don't have to.
I can make my own breakfast.
Watch me.

He begins to go.

Zephyr   I'll do it.

58   Not too runny.
The eggs.

Zephyr   I know not too runny!
She marches off.
He sits there.

58   I stopped. I can do that. I can stop.
The lights fade.

Scene Three

The same living room.
Thirty years earlier.
The house is brand-new. It shines.
Price tags are still on the furniture.
28 *sits cross-legged on the floor.*
Loretta *enters. Played by the same actress.*
Different hair if there's time.
They kiss without thinking about it.
She gives him coffee.
A ritual.
Silence. Shared silence.
She hums a tune to herself.

Loretta   How's your cough?

28   It loosened up.

Silence.
Shared silence.
She hums.

Loretta   I ironed your shirt.

28   The one with the stripes?

Loretta   Yes.

28   Thank you, baby.

Loretta   You're welcome, baby.

They kiss.
More feeling.
More silence.

28   Did I ever tell you about when I sold Bibles door to door?

Loretta   No, because you never did.

28   Sure I did.
You think you're the world's expert on me?

I sold Bibles door to door to pay the bills around the house.
I was only sixteen at the time.
What sealed the deal was my way with people.
Sitting in anonymous homes.
Women too much alone.
They would have talked to a mannequin.
Force feeding me tea.
But one woman, Sally Jankis was her name.
Lived by the sea.
She said she waited for the night.
I asked why.
She said because at night the world grew quiet and gave her
more space to feel.
Remarkable woman.
I would visit her from time to time.
Sitting in shared silence.
The lighthouse going around and around.
She knew everything there is to know about silence.
And with that, I'd better be off.

He begins to go.

Loretta   Don't go yet.
Stay with me a couple of minutes.

28   Okay.

The phone rings.

28   Don't answer it.

Loretta   I have to it could be important.

28   Nobody calls this early except one person.

Loretta   Not necessarily.
Anybody could call at any hour of any day.

She picks up the phone.

Loretta   Hello?
Good morning, Mother.

28   I win.

Loretta   Yes, we're just waking up too.

28   I'm fine.

Loretta   He's fine.

28   Thank you for asking.
What is the weather going to be like?

Loretta   Yes, it might snow later.
That is what they say.

28   Small talk.
Where will this conversation go?

Loretta   I miss him too.
I know how hard you miss him.

28   A slight improvement on the weather.

Loretta   There is no end. There can't be.

28   Words of comfort.

Loretta   Shhhh. Shhhh. Shhhh.

28   She probably just wants to see her blood continue.

Loretta   Shhh. Shhh. Shhh.

28   Every day the exact same conversation.

Loretta   Shhh. Shhh. Shhh.

28   Don't forget to say it.

Loretta   I love you.
And I'll call you later.

She hangs up.

28   Now I do really have to go.

He begins to go.

Loretta   The other day I pulled a muscle crying.

28   Which one?

Loretta   In my back. I don't know its name.

He stops.

Loretta   While I was waiting.
That's what I do.
When you're not here.
I wait for you.

28   You wait.

Loretta   No one taught me how.
I taught myself.
I name the hours as they pass.

28   What are their names?

Loretta   There are the hard hours. The hours you can't bear
your reflection.
The hours you don't notice passing. And there are the hours
you simply have to endure.
But the time passes anyway and I hear the car in the driveway
and then you're home and I feel okay again.

28   Are you okay?

Loretta   Sometimes.

28   Sometimes?

Loretta   I listen to the clock in the kitchen.
That's the only sound in the house with no babies crying or
even the hint of a baby.

28   Are we talking about that today?

Loretta   Maybe we are.

28   It's going to be that kind of day then.

Loretta   I can't forget.

28   Nobody's asking you to.

Loretta   There was supposed to be a baby crying.

A baby cries.

28   There will be again.

Loretta   Is it my fault?

28   It's no one's fault.

Loretta   Did I do something wrong?

28   No.
Baby.

Loretta   Why did it happen to me?
Why?
Why?

28   There is no reason.

Loretta   I can't forget.

28   I can't either.
But it's nobody's fault.

Loretta   No.
You're right.
It's just another day without a baby that was supposed to be crying.

The baby stops crying.

28   Nobody's asking you to forget.

He holds her hard.
She begins to go.

Loretta   I've got to get moving.
I've got a million things to do today.

She gets moving.

28   Stop.

She stops.

28   What about this:
After you do everything you have to do you go to the dress
store.
You buy a new dress and you come home and spend an hour in
front of the mirror getting ready.

Loretta   Getting ready for what?

28   You said you always wanted to hear the symphony.

Loretta   Are you asking me out on a date?

28   I am.

Loretta   Ask me proper.

28   Loretta.
My wife.
Would you like to go out on a date with me?

Loretta   I have to think about it.

28   That's what you said.

Loretta   When you first asked me.

28   We were kids.

Loretta   Who didn't know any better.

28   I didn't know your name.

Loretta   At the Homecoming Dance.

Music rises.
The tune she was humming earlier.
If you want to get crazy maybe a mirrorball descends and spins.

28   I came across the room.

Loretta   Do it again.

He comes across the room.

28   Do you want to dance?

Loretta   I have to think about it.

28   And you did.

Loretta   For three songs.

28   And then you said.

Loretta   Yes.

28   Three letters.
One syllable.

Loretta   Yes.

They dance a little bit.

Loretta   Kiss me like we're happy.

28   I don't have to pretend.

He kisses her.
He checks his watch.
Music dies.

Loretta   Let me make you breakfast.

28   I don't have time anymore.

Loretta   It will only take a couple of minutes.

28   I'll be late.

Loretta   What's a couple minutes?

28   People will talk.

Loretta   Are we in an Ibsen play?
People will talk?
Don't go.
Not yet. Please.
Let me make you breakfast.
I know how.
I know just how you like it.
Have you noticed I lost almost seven pounds?
Have you noticed how happy I am when you're here?
Have you?

28   Baby.

Loretta   Just some eggs.
What's a couple of minutes?
I don't want to be alone. Not yet.

28   Okay.
Just let me get dressed.

Loretta   And then a little breakfast.
To begin the day.

He begins to go up the stairs.

Loretta   And after work you'll come home.

28   I always do.

Loretta   Every day.

28   Every day the exact same homecoming.

Loretta   I listen for the sound of the car in the driveway.
And then I feel okay again.

28   You won't cry today?

Loretta   I'll try not to.

28   Try hard, okay?

Loretta   Okay, I'll try.
And tonight we go out on a date.

28   I've got to get going.

Loretta   I'll spend an hour in front of the mirror.
It will be a glorious evening.

28   Shhhh.
Shhhh.
Shhhh.

He's at the top of the stairs.
88 *enters.*
He watches.

Loretta   Kiss me first.

28   How?

Loretta   We've got to practice.

28   Practice what?

Loretta   Kissing goodbye.

They kiss.
He goes upstairs and she goes into the kitchen.
88 *is alone.*

88   Kissing goodbye.
Yeah.
We got used to that.
I still remember the way her hips swayed.
At the Homecoming Dance.

Music rises.
He dances alone.

88   One two three.
One two three.
A waltz.
And me trying to pretend I wasn't as hard as the rock of
Gibraltar.
Ass out a bit.
Pretending it wasn't there.
One two three.
One two three.

He dances a bit.

Day turns to evening.

It does.
Day turns to evening.

88   Echoes of another day.
Resounding in a silent chamber.
Music finished.

Music dies.

88   And now.

Suzanne *enters with her bag and turns on a light.*

88   Boo.

Suzanne   Jesus Christ!
You scared me.

88   I meant to.

Suzanne   I'm going to get going.

88   Why?

Suzanne   Because I get paid to stay from morning until night.
And it's night.

88   It is evening.

Suzanne   Late evening.

88   But not quite night yet.

Suzanne   Very close.

88   So I'm paying you until night.
Aren't I?
And we can agree it is not night yet.

Suzanne *puts down her bag.*

Suzanne   We can.

88   So you'll stay.

Suzanne   Not very long.

88   Just until the night.

Suzanne   Until then.

88   Good then.

Silence.

88   Did I ever tell you when I used to work at the mannequin factory.
This was before your time, but…

Suzanne   What's your first name?

88   Gustin.

Suzanne   Gustin.
You know.
There's a lot of nice places you could go.

88   Places for old people.

Suzanne   For elderly people.

88   You die quick there.

Suzanne   And what do you do here?

88   Die slower.

Suzanne   My grandmother is in one.
It's very nice.
She's quite happy.

88   Hey, good for her.

Suzanne   They have activities.

88   I don't want to make any moccasins.

Suzanne   What?

88   I knew a woman.
She lived in one of those places.
Her name was Bonnie.
I'd visit her from time to time.
And every time she gave me a pair of moccasins.
Look in the cardboard box over there.

She opens the cardboard box near the window. Moccasins fall out.

88   Have a pair.
Have three.

I don't need them.

Suzanne   I don't need any moccasins.

88   Neither do I!
That's what I'm talking about.

Suzanne   But it might be nice to be around people your own age.

88   They smell funny.

Suzanne   It might be nice to make some friends.

88   I have you.

Suzanne   You pay me.

88   You're saying you're not my friend?

Suzanne   Yes.

88   She's not my friend.
Now she tells me.

Suzanne   Okay I am your friend.
But it might be nice to make friends you don't pay.

88   I can't leave.

Suzanne   What do you mean?

88   What part didn't you understand?

Suzanne   The can't part.

88   The can't.
The I is simple.
The leave.
But the can't.
That's a longer story.

Suzanne   Tell me.

88   I thought you were going.

Suzanne   Please.

88   Can't.
Contraction of cannot.
Can't.
This is the only place on earth that I belong to. So I can't leave.
Simple.
You can go home now.

Suzanne   I want to know the story.

88   Now she wants to know!

Suzanne   Tell me!

88   They're still here!

Suzanne   Who is?

88   Who do you think?

Suzanne   I don't know I met you this morning!

88   My daughter.
My wife.
My wife and my daughter.
They're still here.

Suzanne   Do you see them?

88   No.
I'm not crazy. Not yet anyway.
There are echoes.
Do you know what I mean?
They were here.
And then they weren't.
And I have to stay here.
Because this is where they were.

Suzanne   It's falling apart this house.

88   There are echoes.
And yes it would be nice to know some people my own age
so we could watch *Cocoon* or *Driving Miss Daisy* or something
with Jessica Tandy in it and say, "Wow, we might be old

but we're still alive" and play volleyball or make bird feeders.

Suzanne   My grandmother does not play volleyball.

88   They have classes in those places.
Ceramics with Lori.
Jazzercise with Shelia.
Laugh and Relax with Dr. Daniels.

Suzanne   She made one bird feeder and it's quite beautiful.

88   Fantastic. I would like to engrave her a trophy.

Suzanne   I watch the sparrows and the robins. But now they're all gone for the winter.

88   I can't leave.

Suzanne   I haven't been doing this job for long. But I've seen people who are so lonely.

88   So here's one more.

Suzanne   But you don't have to be.

88   Too late for that.

Silence.
She checks her watch.

Suzanne   I'm sorry, Gustin, but I do have to go.

88   Not yet.

Suzanne   It's night.

88   Who agreed on that?
I did not agree it is night.

Suzanne   It's dark!

88   It is very very late evening.

Suzanne   I've got my boyfriend.

88   Tell me about him.

Suzanne   You didn't care earlier.

88   Now I do.
Now I am deeply interested.
What's his name?
What's he do?
Is he a sensual lover?

She gives in.

Suzanne   His name is Alex.

88   Wonderful name.
I had a cousin named Alex. Half spastic and half retarded.
Shitting himself every other day. But it's a wonderful name for
your paramour.
What's this young buck do?

Suzanne   He's a musician.

88   I love music.
What kind of musician is he?

Suzanne   He plays guitar.

88   Does he sing?

Suzanne   He sings backup.

88   My wife used to hum when she was happy.

Suzanne   He tutors kids.

88   Maybe happy isn't the word.
But not unhappy anyway.

Suzanne   For extra money between gigs.

88   Maybe he could tutor me.
What does he teach?

Suzanne   Algebra, geometry, and calculus.

88   I could brush up on my mathematics.
I remember knowing how to calculate the shape of a curve.

We'll bring the young buck over and brush up.

Suzanne   I'd actually be more comfortable if you didn't meet him.

88   Why? I'm a wonderful conversationalist. I don't drool yet and I know a number of jokes. Have you heard the one about the nun, the priest, and the pony?

Suzanne   I just like to keep my work and my life separate.

88   Okay. So there's a nun, a priest and a pony, and they walk into a bar. The nun says, "I was born illegitimately to a very successful oral surgeon in Tallahassee." And the pony says–

Suzanne   I've got to get going.

88   Just a few more minutes.

Suzanne   Just a few more and then I've got to get home.

88   You're expected.

Suzanne   That's right, I'm expected.

88   Nothing so comforting.
Have you talked about having children?

Suzanne   We talked about it.

88   What did you say?

Suzanne   What do you mean?

88   What do you think I mean?
When you talked about it, about having children, what was said?
What was the nature of discussing life floating downbloodstream?
Is it a daunting concern for him?
The responsibility of the salt of your tears and the red of your blood and the blue of your eyes to live in another soul?

Pause.

Suzanne   We're thinking about it.

88   I know the very night my daughter was conceived.

Suzanne   You know which night.

88   It could have only been one.

Suzanne   Why only one?

88   Because I could feel it.
I took my wife out.
To the symphony.
We heard Beethoven's Sixth.
Her eyes.
Her eyes were so bright.
Brighter than words can carry.
We came home. Had a fight.
The most difficult thing in life is the intimate relationship
between two people.
The second is staging a musical.
But.
We made up.
I held her hand.
She held mine.
We conceived a child. I was a very sensual lover.
Nine months later she died during childbirth.
And I had a daughter and no wife.
But I don't talk about that.

Suzanne   I'm sorry.

88   For what?

Suzanne   Your wife dying.

88   Thank you I feel so much better.

Suzanne   That's it I'm going.

88   I'm sorry!

Suzanne   Look outside.

He looks.

88   Okay. Now what?

Suzanne   What does it look like?

88   It looks like the beginning of winter.

Suzanne   And.

88   It is dark.

Suzanne   And.

88   It looks empty.

Suzanne   And.

88   Silent.

Suzanne   And?

88   Lonely.

Suzanne   Is it evening?

88   Not anymore.

Suzanne   What comes after evening?

88   Night.

Suzanne   Thank you!

88   It has become night.

Suzanne   We agreed.

88   We did.

He takes out his wallet. Gives her money.

Suzanne   This is too much.

88   It's called a tip. Take your boyfriend out. Have a beer on me.

Suzanne   Thank you.

88   Don't play too easy to get.

Suzanne   I won't.

88   But not too hard either.

Suzanne   Right in the middle.

88   And you'll be back in the morning.

Suzanne   I don't see the point.

88   –because I need you to come back.
I need to have something to look forward to.

Suzanne   Okay.
I'll be back in the morning.

88   Thank you, Suzanne.

Suzanne   Goodnight, Gustin.

88   Goodnight.

She goes out the front door.
Gusty.
He looks out.

88   There are echoes.

58 *enters wearing an old suit. It's seen better days.*
He drinks a beer out of a can.
It is evening.
88 *watches.*
Rock music plays upstairs.
Zephyr *comes downstairs.*

Zephyr   Look at you.

58   What?

Zephyr   You put on your suit.

88   The same old lines.

58 and 88   I figured I have one might as well wear it.

Zephyr   Well well well.

58   Don't.

Zephyr   You've never worn your suit before.

88   And never wore it again.

58   I just felt like it.

Zephyr   All the other Bonnies.
They never got the suit.

58   Times have changed.

88   Not exactly.

Zephyr   You won't make her feel self-conscious about her
weight?

58   She looked nice enough.

88   Ha ha ha.

58   What?

Zephyr   I'm just surprised.

58   Let's not get ahead of ourselves.

Zephyr   I'm not.

58   We haven't even met.

88   A night to forget.

Zephyr   I know.

58   Let alone made out or anything.

Zephyr   Making out in your head are you?

58   No. Well,
I don't know.

Zephyr   Times have changed indeed.

88   They never fucking did.

58   I can take care of myself.

88   Ha!!

Zephyr   Okay.

58   I'm serious.

Zephyr   When?

58   When what?

Zephyr   When have you taken care of yourself?

58   You seem to forget, you lady, that I did raise you alone.
Changed your diapers and wiped up your vomit.
Watched your eyes reflect the soul of everything I didn't have.

Zephyr   You had Wanda.

88   Ahh, Wanda.

58   So what?

88   Her hips swayed just right.

Zephyr   Wanda changed my diapers.

58   I don't want to get into an argument about who changed
your diapers.

Zephyr   There is no argument because it was Wanda.

88   I didn't like the smell of shit.

58   I had to work.
So I had a little extra help.

Zephyr   Wanda.

88   Who likes the smell of shit?

58   Yes the help happened to be named Wanda.

88   Perverts perhaps.

Zephyr   And what happened to Wanda?

58   Wanda moved to Florida?

88   Wanda killed herself.

Zephyr   And why did Wanda move to Florida?

58   How should I know why Wanda moved to Florida?
Is it me who is supposed to know why a person moves to
Florida?
Because of the sun.

Zephyr   No.

58   Tax shelters.

Zephyr   No.

58   She wanted to be closer to Disney World tell me then.

Zephyr   Because she was in love with you.

58   She was not.

88   Yes, consumed.

Zephyr   Dad I was twelve and I knew she was in love with
you.

58   Our relationship was strictly professional.

88   We would have a go every couple of weeks.

Zephyr   She opened your beers for you.

58   Somebody had to open the beers why not Wanda?

88   In the laundry room

Zephyr   She worshipped you.

58   Whether she did or not I couldn't say.

88   On lonely afternoons.

Zephyr   You couldn't say?

58   Maybe she had a little crush.

88   She lasted like Thursday.

Zephyr   A crush?

58   Perhaps an infatuation.

Zephyr   A little bit more.

58   Perhaps maybe and I am only supposing maybe she was a little teeny weeny bit in love with me.

Zephyr   Thank you.

88   Not enough room for her. A locked door at the end of a darkened hallway.

Zephyr   And what was wrong with Wanda?

58   She was the help.

88   She wasn't your mother.

Zephyr   She was beautiful.

58   Beautiful help but help all the same.

88   Not the right eyes.

58   And I wasn't ready.
Okay?
It was too soon.

Zephyr   It was more than ten years.

88   Ten years of unforgetting.

58   Ten years isn't that long.
Not for that.
I'm not ready now.
And what am I doing?
I dressed up in this fucking suit.
I'm going out on a date with a fat person.
Does that make you happy?

Zephyr   No.

58   No?

Zephyr   It's not supposed to make me happy, Dad.

88   Happiness.

58   Who is it supposed to make happy?

88   Ha ha ha.

Zephyr   You, Dad.

58   Too late for that.

88   IT WAS NOT TOO LATE FOR THAT YOU DUMB
FUCK!!

Zephyr   You're still young.

58   I can take care of myself.

88   Ha!

Zephyr   Fine.
You just never have.

58   That's not fair.

Zephyr   Fair or not, I've been cooking every meal for you
since I was fourteen.

58   You've gotten much better since then.

88   I can still taste your pork roast.

Zephyr   A teenager is not supposed to cook for her father.

88   I can still smell your hair.

58   Somebody had to cook.
Why not you?

Zephyr   Because I was a kid.

88   I can still touch your face.

He does.
He touches her face.

58   A young woman.

Zephyr   Fine.
A young woman.

88   Your eyes.
Same as your mother's.
I gazed so hard at them.

58   And Wanda left.
Couldn't keep her feelings to her heart.
She felt she had to unburden herself.
Hey, listen.
Thanks, but just cook my dinner and shut the fuck up.

88   Killed herself in a motel outside Orlando.

Zephyr *moves.*
88 *can't touch her face anymore.*

Zephyr   I can't believe you.

58   Look.
Look!
I'm going out on a date.
I didn't even ask for dinner.

Zephyr   Because you're going out for dinner.

58   Right.
I didn't ask for my dinner.

Zephyr   Because you're going out for dinner!

88   Doorbell.

The doorbell rings.

58   I don't want to go.

Zephyr   Dad.
You have to go.

58   She's fat.

Zephyr   She's not.

58   She's not your mother.

Zephyr   Nobody is!

88   Nobody is!
The same old lines.

58   Why are you yelling?

88   Doorbell again.

The doorbell rings.

58   I'm not yelling.
You're the one who's yelling.

Zephyr   Just go.

58   You're not mad at me.

Zephyr   No.

58   Good.
I hate when you're mad at me.

Zephyr   Well I'm not.

58   Do I have to go?
Is me putting on the suit enough?

Zephyr   No.

58   I have to go out.

Zephyr   Yes.

58   And laugh at her jokes.

Zephyr   Even if they're not funny.

58   Did you hear the one about the rabbi, the notary public,
and the albino?

Zephyr   You've already told me that one.

58   They walk into a bar and–

Zephyr and **88**   … and the bartender says, "What is this, a joke?"

58 *and* **88** *laugh long.*

Zephyr   Go!
And pay for everything.

58   Really?

Zephyr   Yes!

58   What if I don't like her?

Zephyr   You pay anyway.

88   Joy's soul lies in moments shared.
Doorbell again.

The doorbell rings.

58   What are you going to do?

Zephyr   I'll find something.

58   It will only be a few hours.
At most.

Zephyr   I won't wait up.

58   I wish we could spend a quiet evening together just the two of us.

Zephyr   We do that every night.

88   A quiet evening.
Shared silence.
A minor blessing.

58   But it's my favorite thing.

88   My favorite thing.

Zephyr   Bonnie.

58   That's her name this time?

Zephyr   That's her name.

58   I know how to be happy.

88   Ha!!

Zephyr   Okay.

58   I do.
I know how.
Just watch me.

Zephyr   Dad.

58   Zephyr.

88   Like the west wind.
Your eyes.

Zephyr   She's waiting.
You're being rude already.

58   Right now, in this light, except for the haircut, you look just like your mother.

Zephyr   Do I?

58   You are the portrait of her.

88 *assesses her.*

88   A portrait.
Eyes.
Hair.
Smell.
All too much the same.

Doorbell.
Knocking too.

Zephyr   Go.

88   Another moment passed.

58   Don't wait up.

Zephyr   Don't worry.
I won't.

58   I was just kidding.
Will you wait up for me?
I won't be late.

Zephyr   Fine.
I'll wait up.

58   So I'll see you later.

Zephyr   You will.

58   Kiss me goodbye.

88   More goodbyes.

She kisses him.

Zephyr   Goodbye Dad.

88   Always more.

58   Goodbye.

88   Goodbye.

He goes. **Zephyr** *is alone.*

He says goodbye to **Zephyr***.*

88   Goodbye.

Zephyr *goes as* **28** *enters in the same suit only newer.*

88 *follows* **58** *off.*

28 *gathers coats and scarves*

88 *(offstage)*
In my mind there was the usual detritus shaking off the day
after the homecoming beginning the night remembering the
day's regrets and views out my window a certain elm tree
swaying the same way in wind still cold enough the world dying
again all the things I did not say living reflections from a dream

another dream of the hours in between back and forth in
between one room and then another each without a memory
of having breathed there most rooms I don't remember but
the problem is nobody ever taught me to forget the chorus in
the courtyard sang the hymns at precisely six o'clock same as
ever familiar enough the singing this part of the earth falling
quickly toward deeper night and not afraid of the dreams to
come but not happy either the body not electric but blood
and a few spaces I won't ask again what silence sounds like the
curtains drawn or not the detritus of the day the homecoming
regret wind dreams hours rooms hymns please put words for
all or some at least of what I know but do not say why I cry but
look away what giggles me in my solitude please let this be the
promised glorious evening please show me the glory of living
please name for me all that I feel but cannot sing.
Please.

Loretta (*offstage*)   Are you ready?

28   For what?

88 *ushers* **Loretta** *in.*

88   And now.
Drumroll, please.
The time of my greatest happiness.

Loretta (*offstage*)   For me to make my entrance.

28   I think I'm ready.

88   Still when there were entrances.

Loretta (*offstage*)   Close your eyes.

He doesn't.

28   They're closed.

88   I'll keep mine wide open.

Loretta (*offstage*)   No they're not.

28   How did you know that?

Loretta (*offstage*)   Close them.

He does.

28   They're closed.

She enters from upstairs with strained poise.
Her dress is brand-new.

Loretta   And she descends the staircase of her new home.
Which they can't afford but live in anyway.
She looks radiant in her new dress.

28   Can I open my eyes?

88   You never will.

Loretta   I have yet to finish my entrance.

28   It is a long entrance.

88   All the best ones are.

Loretta   She takes her time.
She watches her feet.
She sees her husband sitting on the floor as he does.
He looks handsome.

28   Does he?

Loretta   He does.

88   Things change.

Loretta   And she looks radiant.

88   Lights die.

Loretta   The young couple going out for a date.

88   Always young.

Loretta   To the symphony.
Which she had mentioned in passing a couple of times to
which he picked up on so cleverly.

88   You never aged for me.

Loretta   She has put fresh flowers on her father's grave.

88   You always looked just like this.

Loretta   She has cooked her chicken which came out so much better than he expected.

88   In my mind.

Loretta   She has mailed her letters and is ready for a glorious evening.

28   Come on!

88   IN MY MIND!!

Loretta   A glorious evening, out with the man she loves.
It is a portrait then, of two people, very much in love, going out to share a night together.

88   A portrait on a wall in an empty room.

Silence.

58 *enters.*

58   Did I miss the entrance?

88   You did.

58   Pity.
That's one of my favorite parts.

28   Is your entrance finished?

Loretta   It is.

28   I liked it.

58   My greatest happiness.

Loretta   Thank you.

28   I liked the middle the best.

88   I liked the entire thing.
The most beautiful living thing.

Loretta   You can open your eyes.

He does.
She spins.

Loretta   What do you think?

28   You look beautiful.

58   Gorgeous.

88   Too stunning.
Too stunning to say.

Loretta   Do you think so.

28   You've never looked more beautiful.

Loretta   Not once?

58   Never.

88   And never again.

28   Maybe once.

She hits him.

58   Fun and games.

Loretta   When?

88   A little ha ha in a night.

28   The other day.

58   A repartee.

Loretta   What other day?

88   A little back and forth.

28   I'm kidding.
You've never looked more beautiful.

Loretta   That is the correct answer.

58   Two voices.

Loretta   And now.

28   And now.

88   Two voices singing in time.

28   He takes her arm.

58   So close to the end.

Loretta   She swoons.

88   We thought it was the beginning of happiness.

28   She does?

Loretta   She does.

She swoons.
They watch for awhile.

58   The phone?

88   The phone.

The phone rings.

28   Don't.

Loretta   But–

58   Will she answer it?

88   Not tonight.

28   Just for tonight.

Loretta   Just for tonight.

It rings for a long time.
They watch it ring.

58   Filled with hope.

88   That perhaps this feeling will last.

58   It does not.

88   Of course it does not.

No feeling lasts.

58   Some do.

88   No unforgetting.

It stops.

Loretta   Maybe tonight.

58   Shhhhh.

28   Yes.

Loretta   Maybe tonight.
I can forget.

88   Ha!

58   Hilarious.

88   Sort of.

58   No, you're right.

88   HOW WAS I SUPPOSED TO KNOW!?!

28   Maybe tonight.

(*He kisses her.*)

28   And he opens the door.

He does.
Gusty.

Loretta   It is cold.

28   It is the beginning of winter.

Loretta   It is evening.

28   Not yet night.

Loretta   But very close.

28   Very close.
He helps her on with her jacket.

28 *does this.*

Loretta   A simple gesture.

28   Just a husband helping his wife with her jacket.

58   It begins again.

Loretta   Nothing special.

88   Tell them not to go.

28   Nothing special.

58   They can't hear you.

Loretta   And they go.

28   To the symphony.

Loretta   Into the near night.

88   Please.

58   Shhhh.

Loretta   Two people.

88   Please.

58   Shhhh.

Loretta   So very much in love.

88   Please.

28 *makes a grand gesture for her to go first.*
She exits with strained poise.
He closes the door behind him.
The symphony rises as the lights fade.
It rises and rises.
They watch the lights from the window.
Silence as they listen to the symphony.

58   So.
Have you heard any good jokes lately?

88   That this will never end.

58   Not exactly hilarious.

88   This unforgetting.

58   Do you hear me laughing?

88   Haunted by echoes.

58   Because I'm not laughing.

88   No.
It's the least funny joke of all time.

Silence.

58   Well, I'm being rude.
Bonnie's waiting.
I said I was going to the bathroom for a piss.

88   Yes, I remember.
How's the chicken?

58   Above average.

88   The chit chat?

58   Close to sparkling.

88   The dimple?

58   When she smiles.
Maybe I'll check if she has dimples anywhere else.

88   Good luck.
Pause.

58   So, I'll see you later.

88   Unfortunately.
You will.

They hug.
It gets awkward.

88   Yup.

Okay.
I'm done here.

Finished hugging.

58 *goes.*

88 Night again.
Deep night.

The middle of the night.

88 Different than the day.
Emptier perhaps.
More space to feel.
The light from the lighthouse turns around and around.

It does.

88 Showing those the way to come home.
Waiting.
Again.
Alone.
For the mercy of the dawn.
The symphony.
Dies.

It does.

88 Gives way to waves breaking.
A man too much alone.
Dying for company.
Pathetic.
It had to end like this.

The symphony gives way to a car approaching.
The lights from headlights reveal him sitting on the ground in his old
pajamas.
A car stops. Fast.
And there is a knocking on the door.
88 *gets up and gets a baseball bat. He gets ready.*
Puts on his deep trying to be scary voice.

88 (*in a scary voice*)   Who is it?

Suzanne (*offstage*) It's me.

88   Loretta?

Suzanne   Suzanne.

He opens the door. Gusty.

88   Oh why didn't you say so.

Suzanne   Gustin?
Why are you doing that ridiculous voice?

88   Because you never know.

He opens the door. Gusty.
Suzanne *enters in her regular clothes and is very high strung.*

Suzanne   What are you doing with a baseball bat?

88   The neighborhood ain't what it used to be.

Suzanne   Did I wake you?

88   No.

Suzanne   What are you doing up? It's the middle of the night.

88   I was waiting for you.

Suzanne   But I'm not supposed to come until the morning.

88   No. You got here early.

He closes the door.

88   Did you miss me?

Suzanne   No.

88   Oh.

Suzanne   Okay, maybe a little.
But that's not why I came.

88   Then why did you come?

Do you want to hear another joke?

Suzanne   No.

88   Ok, so there's a lawyer, a Hollywood producer, and a blind harmonica player named Old Mississippi Johnson. They walk into a bar and—

Suzanne   We got in a fight.
Do you know what it was about?

88   How many guesses do I get?

Suzanne   None.

88   Was it about why we still use the Electoral College to elect the President of the United States?

Suzanne   No.

88   Was it about how many times the heart can break?

Suzanne   No.

88   No argument there, because the answer is infinitely. Was it about—

Suzanne   —I'm just going to tell you.

88   Okay. That would be easier.

Suzanne   It was about children.

88   About having them or children in general?

Suzanne   Having them.

88   Did you yell?

Suzanne   I yelled.

88   Did he yell?

Suzanne   He yelled too.

88   Did you call each other names?

Suzanne   Yes we did everything you do in a fight.

88   I know well enough what that is like.

Suzanne   He said it was morally unjust to bring a child into this, and this is a direct quote, "into this cock-sucking barren fucking earth."

88   Most days I wish I hadn't been born either.

Suzanne   He said he didn't want to make another mistake. Another quote, "another stain in this world."

88   Yes. Most days I think we're all mistakes.

Suzanne   And he pushed me.

88   Hard?

Suzanne   Hard enough that I fell.

88   Are you hurt?

She rolls up her pants.
Her leg is bleeding.

Suzanne   I didn't know where to go.

88   Let me take a look at it.
It's deep.

Suzanne   It hurts.

88   You need stitches.

Suzanne   I don't want to go to the emergency room. Last time I waited seven hours and–

88   –I can do it.

Suzanne   You can stitch me up.

88   I was a doctor.

Suzanne   When's the last time you stitched someone up?

88   Long enough that this is going to hurt.

Suzanne   I don't mind hurt.

88   Put your feet up and let me get my tools.

Suzanne   You have tools?

88   By tools I mean a sewing needle and some thread.

She lies down and he goes up the stairs which is very difficult.
It's step by step.
Suzanne gets some aspirin and takes it with water from her bag.

88   I'll keep talking so you know where I am.
Here I go up the stairs.
Up.
Up.
Up and up. It's slow going.
And I'm yelling now.
I open the cabinet and take out the tools.
By which I mean a needle and some thread. Some rubbing
alcohol too. For the germs. This reminds me of a time when a
rabbi, a notary public, and an albino all walk into a bar.

Suzanne   No. Please, no more jokes.

88   No, you're right. The time for joking is finished.

Suzanne *checks her phone.*
She doesn't like what she sees.

Suzanne   Motherfucker.

She throws the phone into her bag.

88   And here I come close to the top of the stairs.
Here I come.
Walking down the steps. You can almost hear my joints
creaking.
One at a time.
Step.
Step. What a long trip this has been already.
Down.
Down.
Down.

Suzanne   Okay I get it!

88   I just didn't want you to feel lonely.
I know what that's like.
Okay.
Now I'm here.

Suzanne   Are you sure it's okay that I came?

88   I was waiting for you anyway.
You just got here sooner than I expected.
I have a little job for you. You can sterilize the needle.

He gives her a candle.
She sterilizes the needle.

88   I have a little alcohol swab.
Are you ready?
This is going to sting a little.
And by a little, I mean a lot.

Suzanne   I'm ready.

It hurts.

88   Shhh.
Shhh.

She is in pain.

88   Alright, give me the needle.

He gives her needle and it's really hot.
He screams in pain.

88   Ow! Owww!
It's hot.
Settle down.

He begins to stitch her up.

88   Oops.

Suzanne   Oops?
Don't say oops!

88   It's been a little while.
My hands aren't what they used to be.

Suzanne   Owww.
Jesus.

88   It will be over soon.

Suzanne   How soon?

88   Think of something else.

Suzanne   What am I supposed to think of?

88   A memory.

Suzanne   All I can remember is the time my mother sat
with me in silence for five hours because I wouldn't eat my
vegetables.

88   What a terrible plague memory is.
Tell me about your boyfriend.
How did you two meet?

Suzanne   We met at one of his concerts.

88   That's right he plays guitar.

Suzanne   He sang a whole song and looked me in the eye.
And after it was finished he said that was for the girl in the pink
t-shirt.

88   Were you wearing a pink t-shirt?

Suzanne   Of course I was wearing a pink t-shirt.

88   So the song was just for you?

Suzanne   That's right.
The song was just for me.

88   My favorite poet said this:
You are the song and I practice you
With yellow teeth
A broken tongue

By the field
By the harbor
Even the waves know your melody
Can you hear my voice?
When you are not here
Can you hear me singing in silence?
All finished.

Suzanne   It's all over?

88   All over.
You just have to come back in two weeks so I can take the
stitches out.

Suzanne   Thank you.

88   That'll be four thousand dollars.

Suzanne   I don't have my checkbook.

88   I'm kidding.
For you it's free.

Suzanne   Is it okay if I stay here tonight?

88   There's a spare bedroom.
It was my daughter's.
I change the sheets every week so they'll smell okay.

Suzanne   Why do you change the sheets every week?

88   So I can pretend she's coming home.

Suzanne   I'm so sorry.

88   And tomorrow I'll bring you breakfast in bed.

Suzanne   I'm the one who makes you breakfast.

88   Not until you're better.

Suzanne   When will that be?

88   We'll have to wait and see.
Tomorrow is, after all, another day.

Suzanne   That is what they say.

88   It absolutely had to come.

Suzanne   Tomorrow has to be another day.

88   Let's get you upstairs.
How does it feel?

Suzanne   It hurts.

88   There's some of her pajamas.
I think they would fit you.
Come on.

He begins to go up the stairs gingerly.
She waits at the bottom.

88   Come on.
Let's get you tucked in.

Suzanne   I'm not her.

88   What?

Suzanne   I'm not your daughter.

88   I know but you're her size.
The pajamas will fit just right.

Suzanne   I'm not her.

88   I know that.

Suzanne   And I'm not your wife.

88   I know you're not.

Suzanne   I can't replace them.

88   Nobody can.
Come on.
Let's get you tucked in.
Aren't you tired?

Suzanne   Yes, I'm exhausted.

She cries into his shoulder.
He hugs her.
It's his first hug in a long time.

88   You'll feel better after a good night's sleep.
And it will be better in the morning.

Suzanne   Will it?

88   It can't be worse.

Suzanne   You're wrong.
It can always get worse.

88   I forgot myself.
You couldn't have said anything more exactly true.

Suzanne   You remember how the airline gave you free
tickets to go anywhere with anyone?

88   How could I ever forget?

Suzanne   Maybe you could go somewhere with me.

88   Maybe I could. We'll talk about it in the morning.
Come on. Let's get you tucked in.

Suzanne   Okay.
I'm coming.

She goes up the stairs and they're both offstage up near the bedrooms.
He whispers to her on the way up.

88   One at a time.
There you go.
One at a time.

Just as she disappears **58** *opens the front door.*
88 *sits down and plays a haunting melody on the cello.*
The actress who has no identity at the moment sings the saddest song in the
world.
58 *dances alone, remembering his date with Bonnie.*
After a bit, **Zephyr** *enters.*

Zephyr How did it go?

58 Jesus you scared me.

Zephyr I meant to. How did it go?

58 Fine. You know.

Zephyr Come on. I saw you smooching.

58 So we smooched.
What of it?
And isn't it rude to be spying on somebody smooching?

Zephyr I'm happy for you.

58 It's only a first date.
Can't tell much just yet.

Zephyr But you had a good time.

58 I did. I had the best time I can remember.

Zephyr Well well well.

58 She has the prettiest face and when she smiles there's just this one dimple on the left side.

Zephyr Times have changed indeed.

58 No.
Her left.
My right.
My left.

He tries to figure it out.

58 Either way it is just the cutest thing. Either way for a few minutes I forgot myself.

*During this **Zephyr** has gotten a suitcase from upstairs. She comes down the stairs with the suitcase.*

58 What's that?

Zephyr It's a suitcase.

You put your things in it.

58   Thank you.
What are you doing with a suitcase?

Zephyr   I filled it with my things.

58   Okay I get that part.
Where are you going with the suitcase filled with your things?

Zephyr   Mexico.

58   Mexico?
When the hell were you going to tell me about Mexico?

88 *appears at the top of the stairs.*
He walks down the stairs slowly.
He watches.

Zephyr   I'm telling you right now about Mexico.

58   What am I supposed to do?

88   Suffer.

Zephyr   You've got Bonnie.

58   We went on one date.

88   Drop by drop.

58   It's not like we're in love or anything.

88   Like rain in wind.

58   It's not like I swooned.

88   You will learn the terrors of the human heart in conflict with itself.

58   It's not like I head string music in my head.

Zephyr   I made you meals enough for a week.

58   It was a first date.

Zephyr   They're labeled with each day and each meal.

88   The beginning of the end.

58   We smooched a little, that's all.

Zephyr   You just have to heat them up.

88   Here we go.

58   Maybe just a hint of tongue, nothing more.

Zephyr   After that you're on your own.

58   And what the hell are you going to do in Mexico?

Zephyr   I've never seen the Pacific Ocean.

58   So what?

Zephyr   So I would like to.

58   What's so great about the fucking Pacific Ocean?

Zephyr   I want to know what the tide feels like.

58   I've felt it.
It's not that great.

Zephyr   I called a taxi.
It will be here soon.
I got the last flight out of here.

58   What about the morning?

Zephyr   What about it?
It will come without me.

88   One more attempt.

88 *goes to the suitcase and tries to carry it up the stairs.*

58   Thank you.
I know it will come.
Who's going to make me breakfast?

88   Ha!

Zephyr   I made enough food for a week.

After that you're on your own.

88   An understatement.
Perhaps the understatement of all time.

58   Who will I talk to?

88   You will speak in silence.

Zephyr   I don't care.

58   No.

Zephyr   No what?

58   You can't go.

Zephyr   I didn't ask.

58   I'm still your father.
Aren't I?
Can we agree on that?

Zephyr   We can.

58   I'm your father and I'm telling you you can't go.

Zephyr   You can't tell me what to do anymore.

By now **Zephyr** *has retrieved the suitcase from* **88***'s hands. He gives up.*

88   Another attempt another failure.
Of course a failure.

58   I am telling you young lady.

Zephyr   I'm almost thirty, Dad.

58   That's right you are.
And it's about time you start laying some roots down.
Maybe think about having a family of your own.
I would like some grandchildren.

Zephyr   Dad.

58   What? We could play hide and seek in the house.

88   No more hide and seek.

58   We could play hopscotch in the driveway.

88   No more hopscotch.

He picks up the baseball bat.

58   We could play baseball in the field.

88   They tore up the field.
Put up a parking lot.

58   "Hey there, little Jimmy.
Now, make sure your feet are parallel with your shoulders.
Line your knuckles up.
Stay loose and tight, that's right.

Zephyr   Stop.

58   "Shift your weight.
Twist your hips.
Keep your eye on the ball
Yes, that's exactly right."

Zephyr   Stop it.

58   I WOULD LIKE TO SEE MY BLOOD CONTINUE

Zephyr   DAD.
STOP!

58   I stopped.
I stopped.
I stopped.

88   We've only just begun.

Zephyr   I'm going.

58   Please don't go.

Zephyr   I'm sorry.

58   Are you?

Zephyr   No.

58   Then don't say it.

Zephyr   Okay.

58   I'll be all alone.

Zephyr   You'll get used to it.

58   You're my whole life.

Zephyr   I don't want to be.

58   But you belong to me.

Zephyr   No I don't.

88   Can I get a taxi honk?

The taxi honks.

88   Thank you.

Zephyr   That's my taxi.

88 *goes to the front door and opens it for* **Zephyr** *to leave.*

58   Let's just talk for a couple of minutes.
About anything you want.
You pick the topic.
Or I'll tell your favorite jokes.

88   The old jokes.

58   We could share a good laugh. How about that?

88   The greatest joke is that this will never end.

Zephyr   I'll send you a postcard when I get there.

88   Never.

Zephyr   To let you know I'm safe.

88   Never never never.

She tries to get by him but he tries to take her suitcase.
They struggle.

It opens and clothes fly everywhere.

Zephyr   Goddamnit, Dad!

58   I'm sorry.
I'll clean it up.

He cleans it up.

58   See?
I can clean up.
See what I can do?
I can clean things up.

Zephyr   I know you can.

He holds the dress that Loretta was wearing.

58   What's this?

Zephyr   It's a dress.

58   Thank you.
It's your mother's dress.

Zephyr   I'm taking it.

58   It's not yours.

Zephyr   Whose is it?

58   Hers.

Zephyr   She's dead.

58   Don't you know that I know that?

Zephyr   No.
I don't.

58   I know.
I know she's dead.

88 *takes the dress.*
Dances with the dress.
By himself.

88   One two three.
One two three.
A waltz.
One two three.
One two three.

Zephyr   I wear it sometimes.
I like to wear it.
It makes me feel like her.

58   You never met her.

Zephyr   No.
I didn't.

58   So how would you know what it is to feel like her?

Zephyr   I wouldn't.

58   No. You wouldn't.

Zephyr   No.
I never met her but I get to miss her too.

58   Just leave me the dress.
Please.
And you can go.
Just leave me with something.

Honk.

58   I won't say another word.
Okay?
She goes to leave.

58   Please!

She throws the dress at him.

Zephyr   Fine.
Keep the fucking dress.
Goodbye, Dad.

58   Don't.

She walks into the audience and sits down.
Not in a real seat but on the steps because every dollar counts.

88   One two three.
One two three.
A waltz.

58   Stop fucking dancing.

88   Fine.

He does.

88   And now?

58   The beginning again.

88   Ahhhh, yes.

58   A night to remember.

88   A night not to forget.

58   The beginning of the end.

88   The beginning of unforgetting.

58   Can we stop here?

88   Not by a long shot.
We're just getting warmed up.

58   MAKE IT STOP!!

88   We must break again.

58   Not again.

88   And again.
And again.
And again.
Have you finished your costume change?

The actress has done her costume change in the audience.

ACTRESS   Yes.

88   Are you ready to begin again?

ACTRESS (*to audience member, a man*)   What do you think?
Shall we continue?

AUDIENCE MEMBER   Yes.

Loretta *goes back onstage.*

88   And.
Here.
We.
Go.

58   Not again.

88   Shhhhhhhh.

She gets halfway up the stairs.
28 *opens the door.*
58 *and* **88** *watch.*

28   Baby.

Loretta   Do not baby me.

28   Your arms do not look fat in that dress.

Loretta   But they look heavy.

28   Heavy, yes.

Loretta   Heavy but not fat.

28   There's a difference.

Loretta   And what is that?

28   One is heavy and one is fat.
Two very different words.

Loretta   I don't see the difference.

28   Come downstairs.

Loretta   I'm going to bed.

She goes to the bedrooms.

28   Please.
Baby.
Baby!
Just talk to me.

She comes out in her slip.

28   Baby.
Come on.
Just talk to me.

She marches down the stairs and sits in the chair with a humph.

Loretta   You wanna talk let's talk.
Huh?
I don't hear any words coming out of your mouth.

28   Baby

Loretta   No, really. What is it that you wanted to say?

28   It wasn't a particular conversation I had in mind

Loretta   I'm freezing.

28   Here's my jacket.

Loretta   Thank you.

28   You're welcome.

Loretta   I'm still mad.

28   I'm letting you be mad.
This is me letting you be mad at me.

Loretta   You're not letting me be mad if you're talking about it.

28   So I can't talk about letting you be mad.

Loretta   No.
You cannot.

28   I'll talk about something else.

Loretta   Good.

28   I'll talk about how beautiful you looked tonight.

Loretta   Looked? Looked?
Past tense.

28   Look.
Look.
But there.
At the symphony.
When I held your hand.
Like this.

He holds her hand.

Loretta   You don't get to hold my hand.

She pushes his hand away.

28   But I have to demonstrate.

Loretta   Fine.
You're holding my hand only for the purpose of demonstrating
a point.

He holds her hand.

28   That's the only purpose.
To demonstrate.
And I was holding your hand.
And the music played.
And I looked over.
Like this I looked.
And I saw you.
In the dark.
But your eyes were still bright.

Loretta   How bright?

28   More bright than words can carry.

Loretta   That bright?

28   That bright.
And we were holding hands.
And.
I'd never been happier in my life.

The symphony rises.

Loretta   Never?

28   Not once.

Loretta   Not once.

28   And I knew.
I have known.
That this is the person I will grow old with.
Grow tired with.
Whose eyes I will watch get wrinkled.
Who will be the mother of my children.
And someone will have her eyes.
And I will see her eyes in another.

Loretta   You're going to make me cry.

28   And I thought I hope I die first.
Because I cannot imagine the world without you in it.

88 *walks to* **Loretta** *and touches her hair.*

Loretta   You thought all that just when we were sitting there.

28   I thought all that.

Loretta   Okay.
I'm not mad at you anymore.

28   Good. I hate it when you're mad at me.

Loretta   I belong to you.

28   No, we belong to each other.

Loretta   You can kiss me if you would like.

28   If I would like. If?

88 *kisses* **Loretta** *on the cheek. It is a kiss without a name.*

Loretta   What kind of kiss should it be?

This next line **88** *mouths. So as* **28** *says it* **88** *mouths the words.*

28   One without a name.

88 (*silently*)   One without a name.

Loretta   I'm ready.

28   Let's meet half way.

Loretta   Okay.
We'll meet half way.

They meet half way and kiss.
They kiss deeply.
And it begins to snow outside.
58 *and* **88** *watch the snow and the kissing.*
They know what's going to happen next.
The kissing gets hotter.
And they're on the floor.

Loretta   Not here.

28   Why not?

Loretta   I like our bed.

28   Our bed.

Loretta   Ours.

She looks out the window.

Loretta   Look.
It's beginning to snow.

28   So it is.

Loretta   It's winter.

28   It is.
Now it is winter.

Loretta   It comes every year.

28   It has to.

Loretta   And now it's beginning.

28   Yes.
Now it is beginning.

She kisses him and runs up the stairs laughing.
Al three men watch her bound up the stairs.
By now this ain't close to naturalism.
Please please please direct the shit out the end.

Loretta (*offstage*)   What are you waiting for?

28   Nothing.

88   You could stop right here.

58 *grabs him hard.*
Holds him.

28   Let me go.

58   No.

88   You have no idea how much pain you'll cause.

28   I have to go.

58   You are not going up those stairs.

Loretta (*offstage*)   I'm taking my clothes off!

28   Let me go!

58   NO!!

88   Listen.

88 *slaps* **28** *in the face.*

88   Listen.
Take a walk.
You can do this tomorrow.
Listen.

This seems like the beginning.
I know.
But it's the end.

Loretta (*offstage*)   BABY!!!

28   She's calling me.

88   Walk away!!

58   Please.

88   You want me to beg.
I'm begging you.

28   No.

58   That's what you think.

58 *takes him to the ground.*

88 *stands over him.*

Loretta (*offstage*)   I have forgotten.

58   Listen.

Loretta (*offstage*)   I am ready to begin.

88   LISTEN!!!!

The lights fade as the symphony rises.
The symphony rises and rises.
Until it's deafening.
And then in the black we hear silence shared.